MW01106852

The Thing with Feathers

written and illustrated by

DOUGLAS WOOD

 A Wind In The Pines book

Adventure Publications, Inc.
Cambridge, Minnesota

Dedicated...

To all seekers of the sunrise and bringers of the spring.

Illustrations by Douglas Wood
Book design by Jonathan Norberg with West 44th St. Graphics

10 9 8 7 6 5 4 3 2 1

Adventure Publications, Inc.
820 Cleveland St. S
Cambridge, MN 55008
1-800-678-7006
www.adventurepublications.net
Printed in China
ISBN-13: 978-1-59193-176-8
ISBN-10: 1-59193-176-2

Dear Reader:

Perhaps no beings of the natural world are as inspirational or instructive as the birds. They inspire us through their ability to fly, to soar, to travel, to see the world from on high. And they instruct practically and metaphorically by contending with many of the same life conditions we encounter—storms and hardship, the building of a nest and the raising of young ones, the time to leave a nest and to spread one's own wings, the taking of a great journey.

And of course, birds are simply wonderful to behold—adding music, companionship, color, and beauty to our world.

If "hope is the thing with feathers," as Emily Dickinson so perfectly put it, there are other things with feathers as well. Things like courage, freedom, perseverance, and perspective. Qualities that are personified by the creatures of cloud and sky and tree, our friends and teachers, the birds.

4

Every sunrise is a question,
every song an answer.

Remember . . . the sky is home
as much as the nest.

Courage. Endurance. Persistence.
Good things . . . small packages.

The farther the flight
the farther the horizon.

And what is life itself but flight?
A gravity-defying dance,
danced impossibly, beautifully
In midair . . .

The winds of grace
are always blowing,
but it is up to us
to spread our wings.

Does the red bird worry if he is a
better singer than the thrush?
Is yellow prettier than blue?

Spread your own wings.
Sing your own song.
Find your own way.

The farthest journey
has but one destination:

Your true self.

All who wander are not lost.

For the heart that takes wing,
castles in the air
are just where they belong.

Balance.

The air that sings the song
also supports the wings.
It's the same breath inside and out.

And sometimes when wings
are still, the wind takes
over and takes you
where you need to go.

Every journey begins
and ends within.
The wings must follow the heart.

Sing the old hymns.

January, 20 below.
The strongest are not
always the biggest.

Seek shelter from the storm,
yes . . . but once in a while
just ride the wind.

Sometimes the goal of flight
is just flight.
The journey's goal
is merely the journey.

Earth, sea, sky . . .
Heaven is below us as
much as above.

To the eagle,
all the world's a circle,
with an eagle in the center.

The waterfowl flies through
a world of truth.
Trees, rivers, stars.

And thus he finds his way.

Spring migration. 2,000 miles.
Mate. Nest. Kids.
Fall migration. 2,000 miles.
Pessimists need not apply.

The optimist's secret?
Act as if you cannot fail.

To know the way is not to
know where to go.
It's to know how to go.

Believe in the sun
when it's not shining,
in the stars
when they are hidden,
in Spring's promise
through the winter . . .

And you become
the thing with feathers.